Girlfriend's Guide TO INFERTILITY

A planner to keep you
organized + stay fearless

This planner belongs to:

____

First Edition

Published by Kate Butler Books
www.katebutlerbooks.com

ISBN: 978-1-952725-11-1

Hello FEARLESS ONE!

You might not realize it right now, but you are fearless. You are about to embark on your next step on your journey to becoming a mother. You took the steps you needed to determine how to get there, and now you're moving forward. That takes a lot of courage, even if you don't realize it right now.

I would love nothing more than to invite you into my home, pour you a cup of tea or coffee, and hold your hand through this entire experience. Knowing that's not possible, this journal is designed to help you navigate this journey using various tools for support.

Let me be clear, I am not a medical professional. But I am passionate about wellness, mindfulness, and being a good friend. However, I did consult with the team at RADfertility (Reproductive Associates of Delaware) to help me put this together. They're amazing at what they do and can be found at www.radfertility.com

My wish for you is that this journal gives you comfort on difficult days, helps you prepare for your doctors appointments, inspires you when you need it, and helps you remember that you are not alone.

Xo,

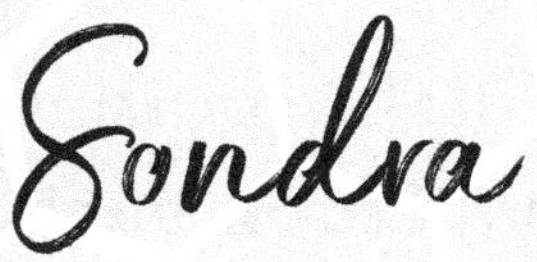

My STORY

My journey with infertility started about two years into my marriage when my husband and I decided that I would stop taking birth control and we were open to receive the gift of a child. Four years later, after rapid weight gain, changes in my skin, inconsistent periods, and ultimately not getting pregnant pushed me to begin looking for answers.

Countless doctors later, I finally found a team that could help me a RADfertility. They uncovered that my right fallopian tube was completely closed, and that IVF was the best option for us to get pregnant.

When I received the diagnosis, I only knew of two other women that had gone through IVF to get pregnant. This inspired me to share my story in the book Women Who Illuminate, and create an online community Fearless Femmes Facing Fertility. I wanted other women to know that they are not alone. That the feelings that they have are part of the process. And where we could share ways that we deal with all of the side effects, emotionally and physically, that come with infertility.

While going through the stages of infertility, I turned to yoga, meditation, and journaling to help keep me feeling like myself during the process. There were times that it was really hard, but knowing that I had these tools to utilize madee the process a little easier.

I'm so grateful that you've invited me into your journey by way of this journal. I hope that it makes it just a little bit easier for you, and **you will look back one day and realize just how strong and fearless you are.**

Planner SECTIONS

Before you get started, here's some clarity on how each section is designed.

DEFINITIONS, TERMS AND ACRONYMS

Welcome to a whole new world of abbreviations, acronyms, and words you never thought you would say. As you start your appointments and talking to others in the infertility community, you will have a better understanding.

GENERAL QUESTIONS TO ASK AT YOUR VARIOUS APPOINTMENTS

Not sure where to get started? These lists of questions can help you through your appointments at key points throughout your journey.

MONTHLY VIEW

Plan out the upcoming month with key dates during your cycle including your appointments. There is a lot to keep track of!

WEEKLY VIEW

Here is where you will start to track your start dates of your cycles, medication and when to take it, milestones and appointments by week. Don't forget to plan time for yourself, your significant other, and your friends as you go through this process.

JOURNAL SECTIONS

Each month will include four journal sections. They will begin with the following:

What am I grateful for? It's important to remember to be grateful. Even if you write down, I got out of bed this morning, that's enough. The more gratitude you give towards something, the more you will receive back.

Affirmation. Affirmations are a way to reprogram the subconscious mind and overcome negative thoughts. There are suggested affirmations for your included in the journal, use them as they are or to inspire you to create your own.

I look forward to... What are you excited about in your personal schedule? A night out, workout class, Amazon package waiting on your doorstep, or a milestone in your cycle.

How am I feeling? It's important to check in with yourself during this process. "How am I feeling" can be both emotional and physical.

Journal. This open space is left for you to write down anything that you want. I found it helpful to get all of my thoughts out onto the page to help me sleep. It is also a way for you to document this process and learn from cycle to cycle.

Section 1

DEFINITIONS, TERMS & ACRONYMS

While this may not be a complete list, this will help you navigate many of the upcoming conversations you will have with your medical team.

AF: Aunt Flow

AFC: Antral follicle count. A transvaginal ultrasound is performed between days 2-4 of your menstrual cycle to look at the number of small (early) follicles on each ovary. This count, along with blood work on day 3 of your menstrual cycle, gives a more complete picture of your ovarian reserve.

AMH: Anti-Müllerian hormone is the best predictor of a woman's ovarian reserve. Higher AMH levels may indicate a better ovarian reserve, but these numbers are used in conjunction with other hormone tests to assess a woman's ovarian reserve. It is ideal to have your AMH checked early in your menstrual cycle.

ART: Assisted reproductive technology such as IUI or IVF.

BCP: Birth Control Pills.

Beta: A beta pregnancy test, is a blood test for the hormone hCG (beta human chorionic gonadotropin). Levels of hCG increase steadily in the early stages of pregnancy, usually doubling to show a healthy pregnancy.

CD1: Cycle Day One is the first day of full flow of your menstrual cycle.

Chemical Pregnancy: Occurs when quant levels are rising as in a typical pregnancy, but there is no evidence of a gestational sac during the ultrasound examination.

DPO: Days past ovulation.

DPR: Days post-retrieval.

DPT: Days post-transfer. Days after an embryo is transferred into the uterus in an IVF cycle.

E2: E2 refers to estradiol which is your level of estrogen. The estrogen level correlates directly with the number of follicles in your ovaries as well as their activity. It helps to estimate how many eggs you may have for retrieval during your IVF cycle. It also helps to indicates if the fertility medications are working the way they should.

Ectopic: A pregnancy in which the fetus develops outside the uterus, typically in a fallopian tube.

EDD: Estimated Due Date

ENDO: ENDO stands for endometriosis, a condition in which endometrial tissue grows outside of the uterus. This can often cause infertility if endometrial tissue attaches to other organs in your abdominal cavity, such as the ovaries and fallopian tubes.

eSET: Elective Single Embryo Transfer

Follicle: A fluid-filled sac on a woman's ovary that usually contains a single egg during her menstrual cycle. During IVF, stimulation with medication can increase the number of follicles that are produced, which should increase the number of eggs retrieved.

FSH: FSH, or follicle-stimulating hormone, is released by the brain to stimulate the ovarian follicles (tiny fluid-filled sacs within the ovary containing a maturing egg) to grow and develop. Your FSH should start in the low range and increases as a woman ages.

HPT: Home pregnancy kit.

HSG: A hysterosalpingogram (HSG) determines the condition of the fallopian tubes and uterus. When an HSG is performed, dye will be placed through the cervix into the uterus and fallopian tubes. An x-ray will determine if the uterine cavity is normal and the tubes are open. This is the best test to look at the tubes and also provides the opportunity to look at the shape and contour of the uterus.

ICSI: Intracytoplasmic sperm injection (ICSI) is a treatment utilized when the quantity or quality of sperm is too poor to effectively penetrate the egg on its own. An embryologist will select a single healthy sperm and inject it directly into the center of the egg.

IM: Intramuscular medications

IUI: Intrauterine Insemination is a low-tech fertility treatment that involves placing sperm inside a woman's uterus to facilitate fertilization. Placing the sperm directly into the uterus makes the trip to the fallopian tubes much shorter, providing the sperm with a shorter distance to reach the egg.

IVF: In-vitro Fertilization is a method of assisted reproduction that involves combining an egg with sperm in a laboratory dish.

LH: Luteinizing hormone (LH) is produced by the gonadotropin cells in the pituitary gland. In women, the rise of LH otherwise known as the "LH surge" is what triggers ovulation, or the release of the eggs.

LMP: Last menstrual period, first day.

MC: Miscarriage

MF: Male factor infertility.

OHSS: Ovarian hyperstimulation syndrome, a rare complication of ovarian stimulation. This occurs when a woman develops fluid in the abdomen and has enlarged ovaries.

P4: P4, or the hormone known as progesterone, is tested to determine many different things: if ovulation has occurred, when it occurs, if there is a normal or ectopic pregnancy, and if there has been a miscarriage.

PCOS: Polycystic ovary syndrome (PCOS) is a disorder in which the ovaries produce excessive amounts of male hormones and the ovaries develop many small cysts. These hormonal imbalances can affect ovulation.

PGT-A: Preimplantation Genetic Testing For Aneuploidies is a state-of-the-art procedure used in conjunction with IVF to select embryos that are free of chromosomal abnormalities and specific genetic disorders, in order to transfer the embryo to the uterus.

PGT-M: Preimplantation genetic testing for monogenic/single gene defects is used to test prospective parents for many different diseases and syndromes. Genetic screening may test for traits that are common in certain ethnic groups that are recessive, or that may have some likelihood of causing serious diseases in affected offspring.

PIO: Progesterone in Oil

PO: Oral medications

PUPO: Pregnant until proven otherwise.

RE / REI: Reproductive Endocrinologist or "Fertility Specialist"

RPL: Recurrent pregnancy loss is defined as two or more consecutive, spontaneous pregnancy losses before the pregnancies reach 20 weeks.

SA: Semen analysis. This must be performed prior to a treatment cycle in order to evaluate the sperm's potential to fertilize an egg. A semen analysis tells your physician the number of sperm that are present, whether they are normal, and how well they move (motility).

SART: This is the primary organization of professionals dedicated to the practice of assisted reproductive technologies (ART) in the United States. On the website, you will find clinic specific information to include success rates.

SET: Single Embryo Transfer

SI: Secondary infertility. This is defined as the inability to become pregnant—despite engaging in unprotected intercourse—following the birth of one or more biological children who were born without the aid of fertility treatment or medications.

Sono (SHG): Saline-sonogram. Thus is performed between cycle days 5-10 to evaluate a woman's uterine cavity. A transvaginal ultrasound is performed once a catheter is inserted into the center of the uterus to instill sterile water, to give optimal visualization.

SQ: Subcutaneous, under the skin injection.

Stimulation: The process of restarting the ovaries once they have been completely suppressed. Medication is taken 1-2 times per day for about 12 days through an injection below the skin on the arm, stomach, or thigh.

Suppression: The process of shutting down your ovaries to prevent your body from ovulating and to prepare your body for the IVF cycle. During suppression, a woman's ovaries are shut down with birth control pills, or medications such as Lupron, Ganirelix, or Cetrotide.

TI: Timed Intercourse. This is the process of monitoring your ovarian cycle via ultrasound, and having intercourse around the time (2-3 days around a positive ovulation indication or at a basal body temperature (BBT) rise)

TTC: Trying to conceive. You should be asked "How long have you been trying to conceive?" People generally consider 'trying to conceive' as the time period in which they have intentionally been trying to have a baby, but physicians consider it to be the entire time during which a couple is having regular, unprotected intercourse.

TWW (2WW): Two week wait. It takes about two weeks from the time a fertilized egg implants in the uterine wall to start emitting enough of the hCG hormone to be detected by the beta blood pregnancy test. After the two weeks have passed you can be reasonably sure that a pregnancy test result is accurate.

US: Ultrasounds. They are useful, not only during ovarian reserve testing, but also to detect abnormalities of the ovaries, uterus, and other structures in the pelvis. You will have ultrasounds not only during the testing phase, but treatment phase as well.

Section 2

GENERAL QUESTIONS FOR YOU TO ASK AT YOUR VARIOUS APPOINTMENTS

Before you even prepare questions, make sure your appointment is a time when your partner can attend with you. They are going through this right along with you and you will appreciate them being there. They might even think of questions that you wouldn't have thought to ask.

FIRST APPOINTMENT

- What specific tests do you suggest myself or my partner to undergo?
- How many REs are part of your clinic? Will you be doing all of my procedures?

AFTER WORK-UP IS COMPLETED AND YOUR TREATMENT WILL BE DETERMINED:

- What are my chances of getting pregnant?
- How long does one cycle typically take?
- How long do I need to wait in between cycles if the first one is not successful?
- Do all treatments require me to take birth control?
- Is there an opportunity to participate in any studies that can offset the cost of treatment?
- What is the difference between a medicated and unmedicated cycle and which is best for me?
- Are there any supplements I should be taking or should stop taking during treatments?
- Please outline all costs associated with treatment. (Your office should be able to estimate the costs and outline what you can expect and you can follow up with your insurance company.)

MEDICATION QUESTIONS

- What is the difference between a pharmacy and specialty pharmacy for fertility medication?

INSURANCE COVERAGE

- It is important that you know what your benefits cover to ensure you understand your potential out-of-pocket costs. Your member services number is listed on the back of your card. Listed below are the most common types of insurance coverage and some questions you may want to review with your insurance carrier.
- Always record when and who you spoke with, as well as the reason and the outcome. It is also suggested that you obtain a written pre-determination of your benefits. This is your most effective tool if you need to challenge a future decision made by your insurance company.
- Please note, that while many Fertility Clinics will help you through this process, the ultimate responsibility lies on you. It is important that you thoroughly understand any benefits you may have to make this process easier.

TYPES OF INSURANCE COVERAGE

- HMO – These plans usually only offer in-network benefits. In addition, you will usually have to provide a referral for any visit.
- POS – These plans usually offer in and out-of-network benefits. However, you may still need a referral in order to maximize coverage.
- PPO – These plans offer both in and out-of-network coverage.

You usually do not need a referral or authorization for these services either, but should always verify this with your insurance carrier.

QUESTIONS TO ASK YOUR INSURANCE ABOUT PHARMACY BENEFITS

- Is there drug coverage?
- Are infertility drugs covered under the pharmacy benefit or medical benefit?
- What is the coinsurance or copayment for drug coverage?
- What prior authorization policies are in effect for medications?
- Are there 30-day drug prescription limits for infertility medications?
- Does the plan pay for self-administered subcutaneous, under the skin injection (SQ) and/or oral (PO) medications?
- Does the plan pay for intramuscular (IM) medications?
- Are there discounts for mail order medications?
- Are infertility specialists encouraged to prescribe one drug over another?
- Can I get a medication that is not a preferred drug or formulary? Can I get a medication that is not covered? If so, am I expected to pay a higher copayment or coinsurance or pay for it completely? And what is that amount compared to the preferred drug copayment or coinsurance?

My NOTES

My MEDICATIONS

Medication Name	Pharmacy Name	Insurance Coverage	Out of Pocket Expense

My AFFIRMATIONS

Affirmations are a way to reprogram the subconscious mind and overcome negative thoughts. I like to close my eyes, take a few breaths, and let my eyes focus on the page. It's my way of asking the universe for what I need to hear at a given time.

I trust
MY BODY TO **CONCEIVE**
AND **SUSTAIN** LIFE.

THERE IS ***no***
PART OF ME THAT
DOESN'T WANT A BABY.

NEW BEGINNINGS
IN MY LIFE.

EVERYTHING
IS HAPPENING IN
perfect
TIMING.

TO **CONCEIVE** A CHILD,
I HOLD
nothing back.

I **CAN'T WAIT** TO
MEET MY NEW
child.

I HAVE THE *best* CARE AVAILABLE FOR **DEVELOPING MY BABY.**

I KNOW THERE IS A *lesson* FOR ME IN THE **PROCESS OF CONCEPTION.**

I DON'T *judge* MY SENSE OF **WORTH** FROM HOW FERTILE I AM.

my body IS **HEALTHY** & **CAPABLE.**

I HAVE SO MUCH *love*
TO GIVE **MY BABY.**

I know
WE ARE **WORTHY**
OF BEING PARENTS.

I AM
open & ready
TO RECEIVE TODAY'S
RESULTS.

I trust

THAT GOOD THINGS
ARE COMING.

YOUR PLANNER

month

notes

Monday	Tuesday	Wednesday

Thursday	Friday	Saturday	Sunday

Monday

Tuesday

Wednesday

Thursday

Friday

Saturday

Sunday

I'm grateful for...

Affirmation

What am I looking forward to?

How am I feeling?

Journal

I'm grateful for...

Affirmation

What am I looking forward to?

How am I feeling?

Journal

Monday

Tuesday

Wednesday

Thursday

Friday

Saturday

Sunday

I'm grateful for...

Affirmation

What am I looking forward to?

How am I feeling?

Journal

I'm grateful for...

Affirmation

What am I looking forward to?

How am I feeling?

Journal

Monday

Tuesday

Wednesday

Thursday

Friday

Saturday

Sunday

I'm grateful for...

Affirmation

What am I looking forward to?

How am I feeling?

Journal

I'm grateful for...

Affirmation

What am I looking forward to?

How am I feeling?

Journal

Monday

Tuesday

Wednesday

Thursday

Friday

Saturday

Sunday

I'm grateful for...

Affirmation

What am I looking forward to?

How am I feeling?

Journal

I'm grateful for...

Affirmation

What am I looking forward to?

How am I feeling?

Journal

Monday

Tuesday

Wednesday

Thursday

Friday

Saturday

Sunday

I'm grateful for...

Affirmation

What am I looking forward to?

How am I feeling?

Journal

I'm grateful for...

Affirmation

What am I looking forward to?

How am I feeling?

Journal

month

notes

Monday	Tuesday	Wednesday

Thursday	Friday	Saturday	Sunday

Monday

Tuesday

Wednesday

Thursday

Friday

Saturday

Sunday

I'm grateful for...

Affirmation

What am I looking forward to?

How am I feeling?

Journal

I'm grateful for...

Affirmation

What am I looking forward to?

How am I feeling?

Journal

Monday

Tuesday

Wednesday

Thursday

Friday

Saturday

Sunday

I'm grateful for...

Affirmation

What am I looking forward to?

How am I feeling?

Journal

I'm grateful for...

Affirmation

What am I looking forward to?

How am I feeling?

Journal

Monday

Tuesday

Wednesday

Thursday

Friday

Saturday

Sunday

I'm grateful for...

Affirmation

What am I looking forward to?

How am I feeling?

Journal

I'm grateful for...

Affirmation

What am I looking forward to?

How am I feeling?

Journal

Monday

Tuesday

Wednesday

Thursday

Friday

Saturday

Sunday

I'm grateful for...

Affirmation

What am I looking forward to?

How am I feeling?

Journal

I'm grateful for...

Affirmation

What am I looking forward to?

How am I feeling?

Journal

Monday

Tuesday

Wednesday

Thursday

Friday

Saturday

Sunday

I'm grateful for...

Affirmation

What am I looking forward to?

How am I feeling?

Journal

I'm grateful for...

Affirmation

What am I looking forward to?

How am I feeling?

Journal

month

notes

Monday	Tuesday	Wednesday

Thursday	Friday	Saturday	Sunday

Monday

Tuesday

Wednesday

Thursday

Friday

Saturday

Sunday

I'm grateful for...

Affirmation

What am I looking forward to?

How am I feeling?

Journal

I'm grateful for...

Affirmation

What am I looking forward to?

How am I feeling?

Journal

Monday

Tuesday

Wednesday

Thursday

Friday

Saturday

Sunday

I'm grateful for...

Affirmation

What am I looking forward to?

How am I feeling?

Journal

I'm grateful for...

Affirmation

What am I looking forward to?

How am I feeling?

Journal

Monday

Tuesday

Wednesday

Thursday

Friday

Saturday

Sunday

I'm grateful for...

Affirmation

What am I looking forward to?

How am I feeling?

Journal

I'm grateful for...

Affirmation

What am I looking forward to?

How am I feeling?

Journal

Monday

Tuesday

Wednesday

Thursday

Friday

Saturday

Sunday

I'm grateful for...

Affirmation

What am I looking forward to?

How am I feeling?

Journal

I'm grateful for...

Affirmation

What am I looking forward to?

How am I feeling?

Journal

Monday

Tuesday

Wednesday

Thursday

Friday

Saturday

Sunday

I'm grateful for...

Affirmation

What am I looking forward to?

How am I feeling?

Journal

I'm grateful for...

Affirmation

What am I looking forward to?

How am I feeling?

Journal

month

notes

Monday	Tuesday	Wednesday

Thursday	Friday	Saturday	Sunday

Monday

Tuesday

Wednesday

Thursday

Friday

Saturday

Sunday

I'm grateful for...

Affirmation

What am I looking forward to?

How am I feeling?

Journal

I'm grateful for...

Affirmation

What am I looking forward to?

How am I feeling?

Journal

Monday

Tuesday

Wednesday

Thursday

Friday

Saturday

Sunday

I'm grateful for...

Affirmation

What am I looking forward to?

How am I feeling?

Journal

I'm grateful for...

Affirmation

What am I looking forward to?

How am I feeling?

Journal

Monday

Tuesday

Wednesday

Thursday

Friday

Saturday

Sunday

I'm grateful for...

Affirmation

What am I looking forward to?

How am I feeling?

Journal

I'm grateful for...

Affirmation

What am I looking forward to?

How am I feeling?

Journal

Monday

Tuesday

Wednesday

Thursday

Friday

Saturday

Sunday

I'm grateful for...

Affirmation

What am I looking forward to?

How am I feeling?

Journal

I'm grateful for...

Affirmation

What am I looking forward to?

How am I feeling?

Journal

Monday

Tuesday

Wednesday

Thursday

Friday

Saturday

Sunday

I'm grateful for...

Affirmation

What am I looking forward to?

How am I feeling?

Journal

I'm grateful for...

Affirmation

What am I looking forward to?

How am I feeling?

Journal

month

notes

Monday	Tuesday	Wednesday

Thursday	Friday	Saturday	Sunday

Monday

Tuesday

Wednesday

Thursday

Friday

Saturday

Sunday

I'm grateful for...

Affirmation

What am I looking forward to?

How am I feeling?

Journal

I'm grateful for...

Affirmation

What am I looking forward to?

How am I feeling?

Journal

Monday

Tuesday

Wednesday

Thursday

Friday

Saturday

Sunday

I'm grateful for...

Affirmation

What am I looking forward to?

How am I feeling?

Journal

I'm grateful for...

Affirmation

What am I looking forward to?

How am I feeling?

Journal

Monday

Tuesday

Wednesday

Thursday

Friday

Saturday

Sunday

I'm grateful for...

Affirmation

What am I looking forward to?

How am I feeling?

Journal

I'm grateful for...

Affirmation

What am I looking forward to?

How am I feeling?

Journal

Monday

Tuesday

Wednesday

Thursday

Friday

Saturday

Sunday

I'm grateful for...

Affirmation

What am I looking forward to?

How am I feeling?

Journal

I'm grateful for...

Affirmation

What am I looking forward to?

How am I feeling?

Journal

Monday

Tuesday

Wednesday

Thursday

Friday

Saturday

Sunday

I'm grateful for...

Affirmation

What am I looking forward to?

How am I feeling?

Journal

I'm grateful for...

Affirmation

What am I looking forward to?

How am I feeling?

Journal

month

notes

Monday	Tuesday	Wednesday

Thursday	Friday	Saturday	Sunday

Monday

Tuesday

Wednesday

Thursday

Friday

Saturday

Sunday

I'm grateful for...

Affirmation

What am I looking forward to?

How am I feeling?

Journal

I'm grateful for...

Affirmation

What am I looking forward to?

How am I feeling?

Journal

Monday

Tuesday

Wednesday

Thursday

Friday

Saturday

Sunday

I'm grateful for...

Affirmation

What am I looking forward to?

How am I feeling?

Journal

I'm grateful for...

Affirmation

What am I looking forward to?

How am I feeling?

Journal

Monday

Tuesday

Wednesday

Thursday

Friday

Saturday

Sunday

I'm grateful for...

Affirmation

What am I looking forward to?

How am I feeling?

Journal

I'm grateful for...

Affirmation

What am I looking forward to?

How am I feeling?

Journal

Monday

Tuesday

Wednesday

Thursday

Friday

Saturday

Sunday

I'm grateful for...

Affirmation

What am I looking forward to?

How am I feeling?

Journal

I'm grateful for...

Affirmation

What am I looking forward to?

How am I feeling?

Journal

Monday

Tuesday

Wednesday

Thursday

Friday

Saturday

Sunday

I'm grateful for...

Affirmation

What am I looking forward to?

How am I feeling?

Journal

I'm grateful for...

Affirmation

What am I looking forward to?

How am I feeling?

Journal

Made in the USA
Middletown, DE
11 April 2021

37392847R00091